Make a
Secret Playhouse

written by Anne Giulieri

photography by Ned Meldrum

To make a secret playhouse, you will need a big box and a *fold-out table.*

You will need some *pillows*, *blankets* and *scissors*, too.

Look for a good place to make your playhouse.
Put the table up like this.

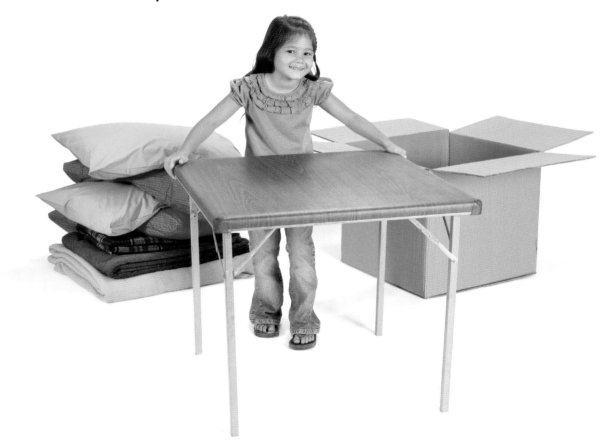

Now, put a blanket over the table, so that you can't see under it. This helps to make a secret place inside your playhouse.

Then get the big box and the scissors.
Cut along the big box, so that it can open
and shut like a *door*.

Next, cut the big box like this.
You will need to cut off all the *flaps*
at the back of the box.

Put the big box next to the table. If you are happy that the big box is in a good place, put the blanket over it.

The big box will look like a *tunnel*
into your playhouse.
To get inside your playhouse,
open the tunnel door.
Then go slowly inside the tunnel
and into your playhouse.

It's good fun to put pillows around the inside of your playhouse.
This will make it soft.

You can take
some *books* and a *torch*
into your playhouse, too.

Look!
Now you have
a secret playhouse.

Picture Glossary

blankets

flaps

scissors

books

fold-out table

torch

door

pillows

tunnel